ANNAPOLIS

A beacon to mariners for centuries,
the Maryland State House rises over
the Annapolis harbor.

The Spirit of the Chesapeake Bay
ANNAPOLIS

KEVIN FLEMING

Foreword by St. Clair Wright

Text by Patricia Barry Kohlhepp

PORTFOLIO PRESS, LTD.
ANNAPOLIS, MARYLAND

First Edition October, 1988, by Portfolio Press, Ltd.

ISBN 0-929518-00-4

Library of Congress Catalog Card Number 88-090924

Any inquiries or orders should be directed to the publisher,
Portfolio Press, Ltd.
P.O. Box 626, Annapolis, Maryland 21401
Telephone (301) 849-8877

END SHEET:
The promise of autumn sailing calls a sloop down Whitehall
Creek as dawn breaks over Chesapeake Bay.

FRONTISPIECE:
Floating docks extend City Dock for the annual October boat shows.

to my wife, Carla, and son,
Jay Penn Fleming,
a native Annapolitan

Preface

For years I have owned a house in Annapolis, but I never really came home. Assignments for *National Geographic* and other photographic projects kept me in the field most of the time.

Then two years ago my life changed; I was going to become a father. Suddenly the idea of foreign travel paled next to the opportunity to stay at home for the birth of my baby.

Luckily *National Geographic* wanted to do a story on Annapolis. After meeting with director of photography Tom Kennedy, the assignment was mine. I was off to discover my own town.

My knowledge of Annapolis was for the most part limited to three obvious subjects: history, sailing, and the U.S. Naval Academy. To make this story work I had to approach the coverage much as I would a foreign assignment. Before I began shooting, I spent many hours interviewing government officials, business owners, artists, craftsmen, and watermen, along with my friends and neighbors. Their insights helped me find Annapolis.

I want to thank the many generous people who showed me their favorite spots in Annapolis, took time to answer dozens of questions, and allowed me to photograph them.

Back at the office my thanks go to *National Geographic* editor Bill Garrett, to Tom Kennedy, and to illustrations editor Bruce McElfresh.

I am honored that St. Clair Wright has written the foreword to my book. Her tireless preservation efforts during the past four decades have helped restore and maintain the character of the old city.

I am thankful to Patricia Barry Kohlhepp, whose picture text has taught me more about my photographs.

Special thanks go to Gerry Valerio for designing the book and pulling the many loose ends together. Thanks also to Jane Vessels, who edited the book. Mame Warren, curator of photographs at the Maryland State Archives, assisted in the selection of the historic illustrations. Her father, the distinguished photographer Marion Warren, developed the sepia prints.

New assignments will again take me away from Annapolis, but coming home will have a new meaning.

KEVIN FLEMING

History
Takes the Helm

BY ST. CLAIR WRIGHT

ANNAPOLIS IS A MUSEUM WITHOUT WALLS, a living landmark three centuries in the making. It has rightly been called "the most individual small town in the entire country."

The capital of Maryland was already considered an "Ancient City" in 1783, when the Continental Congress met in the State House and for nearly a year made Annapolis the capital of the United States as well. Today the small-town city sparkles with the vitality and exuberance of a place loved and tended by generations. In the pattern of its narrow streets, in its architectural diversity, in its roles as a government and maritime center, Annapolis displays a rich blend of continuity and change that was set in motion in 1694 when Royal Governor Sir Francis Nicholson began "his endeavour to make a town of that place."

In 1649 Puritans from Virginia settled this land that lies at the meeting of the Severn River and the Chesapeake Bay. Their first settlement, Providence, lay across the river from the fair harbor settled in 1650 and known variously as Proctor's Landing, Arrundell Town, or Anne Arundel Town—after the wife of Lord Baltimore, proprietor of the Province of Maryland. The town had 200 residents when Governor Nicholson moved the capital from St. Mary's City in 1694. The new capital was soon renamed Annapolis to honor Princess Anne of England. As Queen Anne, she granted the city's charter in 1708.

Drawing on European ideas, Governor Nicholson designed the baroque street plan Annapolis displays today. Streets radiated to the water's edge from traffic circles around the State House and St. Anne's Church. The only land access to the peninsular city was West Street, which passed through palisade gates that were locked each night. Beyond the palisade, a moat separated Annapolis from the wilderness.

FROM THE STATE HOUSE Governor Nicholson and his subjects enjoyed a glorious vista of shining waters and white sails. In 1769 a customs officer named William Eddis reported that this site "commands a variety of views highly interesting; the entrance of the Severn, the majestic Chesapeake, and the eastern shore of Maryland, being all united in one resplendent assemblage." Today the governor, townspeople, and tourists can look out on a remarkably similar scene. The ships are no longer early-18th-century English vessels risking attack by French privateers as they sail between the haven of Annapolis Roads and the Virginia Capes. Nor are they the ships of patriots braving the British blockade during the American Revolution. Gone also are most of the skipjacks, those functionally elegant workboats that once plied the Chesapeake Bay for oysters. Instead, the boats might be sailing yachts preparing for the prestigious Annapolis-to-Bermuda Race, or any of the variety of pleasure boats drawn to this major East Coast maritime center. The scene would still delight William Eddis, who wrote: "Vessels of various sizes and figures are continually floating before the eye; which, while they add to the beauty of the scene, excite ideas of the most pleasing nature."

But this view of the harbor would today be hidden behind a clutter of incongruous high-rise buildings had it not been for the determined and persistent preservation efforts of Historic Annapolis, Inc. In 1952 this nonprofit educational organization launched a multidisciplinary program to aggressively preserve the city's past and help adapt it to modern living. Historic Annapolis has been the driving force behind the restoration of 70 buildings, assisted in the preservation of 400 others, and sponsored research programs and archaeological excavations that have shed light on the city's early days. Appropriately for

Marching from the State House down Maryland Avenue, a parade of unknown celebration drew a crowd at the turn of the century.

this seaport, the first building purchased and renovated by Historic Annapolis was a tavern. Built in 1713 by Edward Smith on what was then Carrolls Alley, this Pinkney Street tavern, or ordinary, is now known as the Shiplap House for its three types of overlapping wood siding, a style more common to ships than to houses.

In 1965 the heart of the old city was named a Registered National Historic Landmark by the U.S. Department of Interior. By a two-to-one margin in 1968, Annapolis voters surprised opponents of preservation by adopting an enforceable historic-district ordinance.

Thanks to these appreciative residents, Annapolis remains a most delightful place for walking. Within the one-third-square-mile area of the Historic District lies the country's greatest concentration of pre-Revolutionary buildings. The district contains 1,500 significant structures dating from 1675 to 1930. Over time, footpaths, lanes, and alleys have naturally grown up between neighboring properties, adding another dimension to the master baroque street plan. Seventeen architectural styles—unorchestrated yet harmonious—can be found along the narrow, human-scale scale streets. Glimpses of the waterfront, hidden gardens, intricate iron fences, gates, and balconies delight the eye.

The flavors of the past have not been lost in accommodating the needs of today. The 18th- and 19th-century buildings, once the realm of inn keepers, shipwrights, ironmasters, clock makers, gunsmiths, music masters, and cordwainers (as shoemakers were known) have been reborn as restaurants, art galleries, offices, clothing stores, specialty shops, boat-chartering agencies, and ship-chandler stores.

The waterfront, shunned as dirty and obsolete even into the 1960s, is now lit with replicas of the city's 18th-century tobacco-leaf lanterns. Tobacco was one of the principal cash crops of colonial Tidewater Maryland, grown profitably with slave labor. "Golden orinoco," Maryland's prize tobacco, was brought to Annapolis for inspection and shipment abroad. The small amount of leaf brought to the capital by less affluent planters was collected and compacted—or prised—into hogsheads in warehouses such as the Tobacco Prise House on Pinkney Street at the corner of Market Space. The great wealth generated in the colony by exporting tobacco, iron, and lumber, by importing British goods, and by selling land brought an era of affluence to the rapidly growing capital after the mid-18th century Political power was the city's magnet, drawing plantation owners, ambitious lawyers, and astute merchants into lively social and economic interaction.

Masterpieces of Georgian architecture, built with as much elegance as colonial technology permitted, rose with the city's fortunes during this golden era. Six of these mansions are listed as Registered National Historic Landmarks. "Their assemblage in one place provides an historical record of an era unequaled anywhere," Baltimore architect Henry Powell Hopkins wrote in 1959. They boast, he felt, "a variety which clearly shows the freedom of their designers in combining motifs pleasantly." The men for whom these showplaces were built left their mark on the history of Annapolis and the country.

The 37-room William Paca House on Prince George Street was the first Palladian-style villa built in Annapolis. Paca completed his home in 1765, the year British Parliament passed the hated Stamp Act. This "taxation without representation" stirred the young lawyer into political action. Paca went on to serve in the Continental Congress, sign the Declaration of Independence, and serve three terms as Maryland's governor. The William Paca House was encompassed by a 200-room hotel when Historic Annapolis, Inc., saved the mansion from demolition in 1965 and began painstaking restoration. Research by Historic Annapolis helped the state re-create the two-acre garden, again a beautiful ornament in the center of the capital.

A mansion of great dignity in both exterior and interior architecture, the Chase-Lloyd House at King George Street and Maryland Avenue was begun in 1769 by Samuel Chase, a young attorney and future signer of the Declaration of Independence who rose to become a justice of the U.S. Supreme Court. In 1771 Chase sold the mansion, unfinished, to Edward Lloyd IV, an Eastern Shore planter whose affluent life-style earned him the nickname "the Magnificent." Though the house strongly reflects the neoclassical style popularized by the English architects Robert and James Adams, it also possesses an opulence of design suited to Lloyd. Particularly notable is the splendid entrance hall embellished with Ionic columns; a monumental staircase rises without visible support to a landing ornamented with a hand-

The architectural beauties of 18th-century Annapolis aged gracefully into the 20th. Completed in 1774 for Matthias Hammond, the Hammond-Harwood House was home to Hester Ann Harwood when photographed about 1910 (left). She was the last private occupant of the house and died here in 1924. Not until the 1940s, when it became a museum, was the house wired for electricity.

The 1765 William Paca House had been expanded and transformed into the Carvel Hall Hotel when this photograph was taken after 1902. It was an elegant social center for the city and conveniently located to the United States Naval Academy. "Here the mothers and sisters of graduating students come," observed a visitor in 1917, "and from it go joyous girls to the dances at the Academy."

MdHR G 1406-001

MdHR G 985-152

Looking down on Annapolis, probably from a hot-air balloon, Baltimore artist Edward Sachse mapped the city in 1863 (top). Civil War hospital tents line the grounds of St. John's College and the Naval Academy, which had been moved to Rhode Island to escape Confederate influence.

Still standing at the head of City Dock today, the 1858 Market House was nearly 30 years old when these farmers brought produce to sell (above).

A panorama of Spa Creek (above, left) taken in 1901 or 1902 captures skipjacks and other craft docked in Eastport, then an independent village. The rectory of St. Mary's Roman Catholic Church stands across the harbor at right. To its left is the Severn Boat Club, today's Annapolis Yacht Club.

Between 1889 and 1892, an unknown photographer climbed into the State House dome and centered his view of the small but densely populated city on Cornhill Street (left).

MdHR G 1890-3890

some Paldian window. Architects William Noke and William Buckland both worked on the Chase-Lloyd House.

Buckland also lent his genius to the neighboring Hammond-Harwood House. The extraordinary talents of this architect, joiner, and carver produced a building so graceful that no owner has ever wished to alter its matchless architecture. A superb example of a Palladian five-part villa, the house was completed in 1774 for Mathias Hammond, a tobacco planter, legislator, and patriot. The loving care of the Hammond and Harwood families has preserved the house exactly as it left the builder's hands. In 1926 auto magnate Henry Ford planned to move the house to Deerfield Village, Michigan. The Hammond-Harwood Association was formed to buy the house and keep it in Annapolis. Today the mansion contains an exceptional collection of 18th-century Maryland furniture.

Merchant and landowner James Brice built his house at Prince George and East Streets between 1767 and 1775. It is the largest Georgian mansion in Annapolis and one of the most impressive brick buildings in American Georgian architecture. The severe exterior of the James Brice House leaves one unprepared for the sheer exuberance of the rococo interior, testimony to the wealth of the era.

The Peggy Stewart House on Hanover Street is a privately owned residence not open to the public. Soon after Peggy Stewart's father, merchant Anthony Stewart, bought the house in 1774 he ran afoul of the political sensibilities of the time: He imported and paid tax on British tea. "From an anxious desire to preserve the public tranquility, as well as to ensure his own personal safety," Stewart apologized to Annapolis and ignited the Maryland Tea Party by personally burning the cargo and his brigantine *Peggy Stewart*. He soon moved his family to England. The house was later purchased by Thomas Stone, a member of the Continental Congress and signer of the Declaration of Independence.

The fourth Maryland signer of the Declaration of Independence, Charles Carroll of Carrollton, owned a great house in Annapolis on Spa Creek; its terraced gardens fall to the water's edge. Now under restoration, the house was first built in the 1720s.

The great houses of Annapolis in private ownership are open to the public only on special occasions. But these architectural treasures of elegant proportions and beautiful details can be viewed from public thoroughfares.

RISING ABOVE THE CITY, Maryland's splendid State House, is the oldest state capitol in continuous use. Constructed between 1772 and 1779, it is the third statehouse to occupy this site.

Here the Continental Congress convened when the British surrendered in the fall of 1783. "The spectators all wept, and there was hardly a member of the Congress who did not drop tears," a Maryland delegate wrote of the ceremony when Commander-in-Chief General George Washington resigned his commission in the Old Senate Chamber on December 23, 1783. Within a month the Congress here received the Treaty of Paris, the document of peace signed in France by the U.S. and Great Britain.

The State House displays Maryland Archives exhibits that depict Annapolis during the Revolutionary War. One of particular interest identifies the still-standing buildings that housed those courageous patriots who represented the thirteen American colonies in the Continental Congress. This is dramatic proof of the survival of original pre-Revolutionary structures in Annapolis.

The Continental Congress adjourned in August of 1784, and — despite lobbying by the leading Annapolitans—the nation's capital moved elsewhere. The business of governing Maryland became Annapolis's economic lifeline as deep-harbor Baltimore lured away the city's commerce and population. But travelers, diplomats, and military visitors found Annapolis a convenient port to Washington, D.C., and officials from the North and the South continued to meet in this central location on the Atlantic Seaboard. The *Maryland Gazette*—described by the late state archivist Dr. Morris Radoff as "the most informative of Colonial newspapers"—maintained its reporting standards. Its pages recounted the city's economic changes; news of clubs, concerts, and theatricals; essays and poems.

MdHR G 1890-3768

The U.S. Naval Academy class of 1888 gathered for a graduation portrait around the legendary statue of Tecumseh.

Commissioning Week was called June Week in 1890 (left), when a young woman chosen by the academy's top company presented the flag in the color-girl parade. The band had yet to strike up its most famous tune: "Anchors Aweigh" was not written by academy bandmaster Lieutenant Charles A. Zimmerman until 1906.

During 1817 and 1818 the *Gazette* reported the city's efforts to persuade Washington to replace old Fort Severn with a new military depot. Success came in 1845 when U.S. Navy Secretary George Bancroft established the Naval School at Fort Severn. Renamed the United States Naval Academy five years later, the school gave Annapolis a much needed financial boost. A Registered National Historic Landmark, the academy embraces one of the largest collections of Beaux Arts-style buildings in the U.S. They were designed by Ernest Flagg and raised early this century when President Theodore Roosevelt gave orders to enlarge the school. Maritime motifs enliven ceilings, cornices, doorways, and balconies. Neptune raises his trident on a handsome door knocker. Other buildings sport sea denizens, shells, birds, and ancient sailing vessels.

The green, open grounds of the academy are a pleasure to stroll in any season. Stately trees line Lovers Lane, and monuments commemorate historic ships and naval battles. The academy is still a tonic to Annapolis, which responds enthusiastically to the lively music of military parades and to the white sails of the academy's fleet on the Severn River.

ANNAPOLIS HAS ALWAYS drawn strength from the water. Generations of watermen have brought catches of crabs, oysters, and fish to its docks. Eighteenth-century guests praised the "fine fish and Delightful Oysters" served on the city's tables.

A model of the waterfront of 1750-1790—when the city was Maryland's principal seaport—is displayed in the maritime museum run by Historic Annapolis, Inc., in the Victualling Warehouse on Compromise Street. Compromises were indeed necessary to resolve the many property disputes that arose when this land on Spa Creek was filled in in the late 19th century.

Shipbuilding was one of the city's earliest industries, though it had all but ended at the time of the Revolution. In the 20th century elegant wooden yachts were built across Spa Creek in Eastport, notably by John Trumpy & Sons, who also produced PT boats for the Navy during World War II. Though only one boat-building company remains in the capital,

the city teems with marine businesses supplying the needs of a growing number of sailors and powerboat enthusiasts. The prosperity is welcomed, yet the "old days" live on in the dreams of Eastporters and Annapolitans and who remember workboats with picturesque sails and still search for yards in which to build wooden ships.

About 1,200 people lived in Annapolis when the United States won independence. Today the population of greater Annapolis reaches 155,000, though only 34,000 people live within the narrow city limits. To acquaint the many newcomers with the city's past, Historic Annapolis, Inc., sponsors tours, seminars, and exhibits, and teaches preservation techniques.

Defending the city's historic treasures against rapacious development is the primary mission of Historic Annapolis. Buildings designated as Registered National Historic Landmarks are not necessarily protected by federal or state law. Local efforts, persistence, and ingenuity are needed to guard these tangible reminders of the nation's history. It is Annapolitans themselves who maintain the look and spirit of a city that can be hailed as it was in the 18th-century: "the genteelist town in North America."

ANNAPOLIS

A channel marker doubles as an
osprey's home. Roosts to more than
80 percent of the Chesapeake Bay's
ospreys, markers were recently
remodeled by the Coast Guard to
keep the large nests from obscuring
navigation lights.

Living with history, residents of Fleet Street maintain houses built by middle-class tradesmen in the late 1700s, a prosperous era when Annapolis was praised as "the genteelist town in North America."

Witness to the marriage of the Severn River and Chesapeake Bay, Maryland's capital city still displays the baroque street plan designed in 1696 by Royal Governor Sir Francis Nicholson. Streets radiate from the city's highest elevation, reserved for the Maryland State House, the oldest state capitol in continuous use (preceding pages).

The seasons of Annapolis unfold on Prince George Street, where architectural styles span three centuries. A puzzle for preservationists, this colonial house (right) may have been built for John Brice III, a lawyer who died in 1766. It is commonly called the Edward Dorsey House, though Dorsey is now known never to have lived in it. Enlarged in the late 19th century, the house is owned by St. John's College. A house may have stood on this site in 1694, when the capital of the Province of Maryland was moved from St. Mary's City. The rough settlement of Anne Arundel Town, named for the wife of Lord Baltimore, was soon rechristened Annapolis in honor of Princess Anne of England.

An English tradition, May baskets bloom on the first of the month on homes and businesses, including the Farmers National Bank (above).

"The wealthiest personages in the State . . . have preferred to reside in Annapolis," a foreign visitor reported in the latter 18th century, when the capital enjoyed a golden age. Drawn by its political importance, lawyers, merchants, and planters grown wealthy on tobacco made Annapolis "the Paris of America," wrote Charles Carroll, who later signed the Declaration of Independence. Another Annapolis signer was lawyer William Paca, who completed his 37-room Georgian mansion in 1765. In 1965 it was rescued from demolition by Historic Annapolis, Inc. The Prussian-blue parlor and its garlanded fireplace mantel (above) emerged from under 22 layers of paint and wallpaper. A hotel, parking lot, bus station, and heating plant once covered the two-acre garden, restored to its colonial elegance (left).

Five generations of William Paca descendants gather on the Chinese Chippendale bridge in their ancestor's garden. Paca served three terms as governor of Maryland and helped ratify the U.S. Constitution. Facing Prince George Street, two blocks from the State House, the William Paca House is one of six colonial mansions in Annapolis designated as Registered National Historic Landmarks.

Another is the Hammond-Harwood House, where a doll once owned by Anne Proctor is displayed beneath her portrait. Renowned artist Charles Willson Peale painted the six-year-old Baltimore girl in 1785. One of the finest examples of Georgian architecture in the U.S., the Hammond-Harwood House owes its beauty to the genius of architect William Buckland. He completed the house in 1774 for planter Mathias Hammond, who never lived in it. The last occupant of the home, Hester Ann Harwood, was a descendant of Buckland.

Power lines vanish in artist Moe Turner's view of an 18th-century barber-shop at Fleet and Cornhill Streets. That vision suits preservationist St. Clair Wright (above), lobbying to bury all utility wires in the Historic District. A founder and now chairman emeritus of Historic Annapolis, Inc., she helped establish the heart of the old city as a National Historic Landmark in 1965. Saved from demolition and adapted for 20th-century living, the buildings in this one-third-square-mile area represent 17 architectural styles from 1675 to 1930 (preceding pages).

"A small elegant lodge," is what Governor Horatio Sharpe envisioned when he began to build Whitehall in 1764. Overlooking Whitehall Creek northeast of Annapolis, the Palladian villa was a country retreat for Sharpe, a popular and farsighted executive who held office from 1753 to 1769 as the city's age of affluence began.

Testimony to that wealth, the Palladian door of the Hammond-Harwood House has been acclaimed by art historian William H. Pierson, Jr, as "one of the loveliest in all of colonial America." The fortunes of Annapolis declined after the Revolutionary War as the city lost commerce and population to a deep-harbor rival up the Chesapeake: "The Capitalists," a traveler noted in 1797, "go and reside in Baltimore."

A handful of history gathers artifacts from excavations throughout the Historic District: a brass keyhole escutcheon, a 1734 glass bottle seal, a bone whistle, a brass thimble, a ceramic tobacco pipe, a Chinese porcelain plate fragment, a lead-glass decanter stopper, a round bone seal, and a 19th-century bone toothbrush. In the background archaeologists from the University of Maryland probe the grounds of the Charles Carroll Mansion, first built in the 1720s. Archaeologists Elizabeth Reed and Paul Shackel examine the tomb of Margaret Chew Bordley (above), discovered during a tree planting at St. Anne's Episcopal Church. A member of one of the town's richest families, she died in 1773 at age 38.

Pricey real estate today, Cornhill Street (following pages) was modestly developed by middle-class merchants and craftsmen during the 18th and 19th centuries.

Shore to ship service, water taxis deliver passengers, newspap

even pizzas to boats anchored in the Annapolis harbor.

"Ego alley," the channel into City Dock becomes a congested promenade as boats of all descriptions jockey to see and be seen—and to beat the odds on finding a slip.

Preserved as part of the Historic District, buildings along the waterfront house a variety of restaurants and shops. On the site of the gabled Middleton Tavern, at far left, tavern keeper Samuel Horatio Middleton launched his business in the early 1700s. He also rented boats and ran a ferry service.

Still catering to visiting sailors, McGarvey's Saloon owner Mike Ashford watches Walter Cronkite autograph the sleeve of oyster shucker Charlie Snowden (above).

All's fair in love and water-pistol war at City Dock, where a dinghy turns into a swimming pool after a day on the Bay. With its superb waters and rich history, Annapolis attracted 4.5 million visitors in 1987.

At the helm of the Annapolis Yacht Club, recent commodores Arnold C. Gay and C. Gaither Scott and current commodore Franklin K. Peacock (left to right) stand before trophies presented yearly to club racing winners. "To encourage and foster the sport of yachting," the club hosts competitions from beginner to expert, including the celebrated Annapolis-to-Newport Race. The season never ends for sailors who brave the club's Frostbite Series (right). All hands on deck must keep all feet in the cockpit to reduce the risk of going overboard during this winter event.

In the glow of a summer Chesapeake evening (preceding pages), sailboats fly wind-catching spinnakers in the Wednesday-night races sponsored by the Annapolis Yacht Club.

Passing the silhouette of the Chesapeake Bay Bridge, a crab boat heads out at dawn. Less affected by pollution than are oysters, blue crabs have become the Bay's top seafood harvest.

With a bushel of fish to re-bait his crab pots and a keg of hydraulic fluid to recharge his engine, a Chesapeake waterman makes his rounds (left).

"Officer, which way to the crab feast?" Outside the Navy-Marine Corps Memorial Stadium a Chesapeake Bay mascot jokes before the annual July Annapolis Crab Feast. Sponsored by the Annapolis Rotary Club, it is believed to be the world's largest. Backstage, volunteers hustle to serve 19,000 steamed blue crabs.

"Beautiful swimmer" is the translation of the blue crab's scientific name, *Callinectes sapidus*. Several times between spring and fall the growing crab sheds its protective coat. Backing out of a shell now too small for its body, a "buster" (above) is soon free. Unprotected for about 24 hours before a new shell begins to form, the prized soft-shell crab is cooked and eaten whole.

The ritual of catching, steaming, and picking blue crabs begins in the spring, when they emerge from winter hibernation in the Chesapeake's bottom mud. At the 1987 Annapolis Rotary Club Crab Feast, some 2,400 people picked their way through 300 bushels (left).

The summer joys of crabbing, fishing, and picnicking mingle on Walnut Creek, a tributary of the South River.

Chesapeake Bay watermen (preceding pages) wait for dawn, the legal starting time for oystering. About four miles wide at Annapolis, the estuary was described by Baltimore writer H. L. Mencken as "a great big outdoor protein factory." But pollution and the devastating oyster disease MSX have reduced the catch of oysters and some fish. With the slogan "Save the Bay," the Annapolis-based Chesapeake Bay Foundation lobbies for massive cleanup.

Gracefully marking the entrance to the South River since 1875, the Thomas Point Light

last manned lighthouse on the Chesapeake before the Coast Guard automated it in 1986.

The world's largest college dormitory, Bancroft Hall houses the 4,500 students of the United States Naval Academy. Named for U.S. Navy Secretary George Bancroft, who began the school in 1845, the hall covers 32 acres and contains four miles of corridors.

It's good luck to toss pennies into the quiver of Tecumseh, a bronze model of a ship's wooden figurehead. In academy lore, midshipmen with accurate aim are guaranteed a passing grade on an exam.

Rigged as a training ship (preceding pages), an Argentine Navy vessel pays a call on the academy. To port, the Aegis guided-missile cruiser U.S.S. *Mobile Bay*, commissioned into the U.S. Atlantic Fleet in 1987, visits to train midshipmen.

When the temperature is at least 55 degrees and the weather is clear, midshipmen

practiced formation in Bancroft Hall's Tecumseh Court before their noon meal.

54

A slippery rite of passage marks the end of freshman year for fourth class midshipmen, called plebes. Muscles strain as a human pyramid (preceding pages) grows around the Herndon Monument, greased with 200 pounds of lard and crowned with a "dixie cup" hat worn by plebes. Tradition has it that whoever scales the obelisk and places an upperclassman's hat on top (above) is destined to become the class's first admiral.

A leafy sentry stands before the dome of the Naval Academy Chapel. Rising nearly 200 feet, the inter-denominational chapel was dedicated in 1908. Tiffany stained-glass windows honor naval heros. The Beaux Arts-style chapel also holds the crypt of Revolutionary War naval officer John Paul Jones, credited with the phrase, "I have not yet begun to fight."

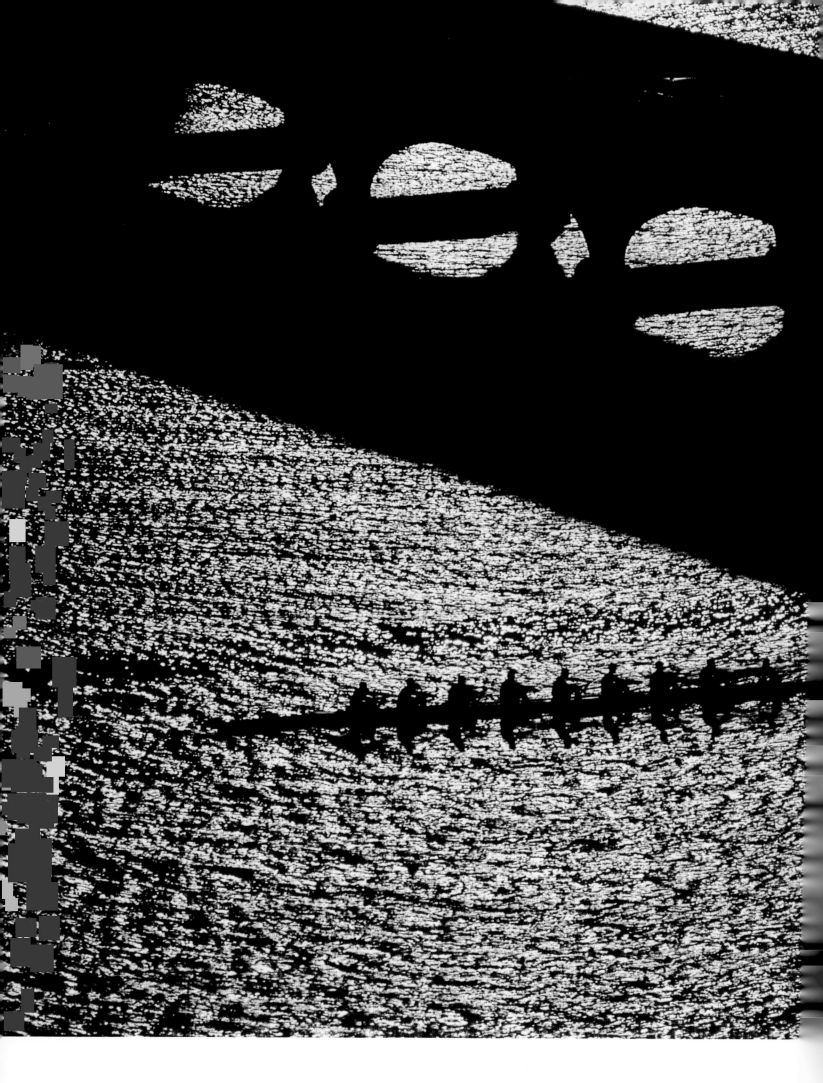

Sunset shadows lengthen as a Naval Academy crew glides past the Severn River drawbridge.

A sea of plebes gathers for a swearing-in ceremony, the beginning of four years of academic and military discipline designed to train officers for the Navy or Marine Corps.

Seated before a painting of the Blue Angels, the Navy's precision flying team, an incoming plebe receives an Induction Day haircut. At City Dock a second class midshipman visits with Annapolitans who march to a different drum.

61

Meeting the Naval Academy's athletic requirements, midshipmen lacrosse players practice on the school's artificial-turf field. Women were first admitted to the academy in 1976 and now account for 8 percent of the enrollment.

Heat topples a midshipman (following pages) during a dress parade competition among the 36 companies of the Brigade of Midshipmen.

Waltz parties are a tradition at St. John's College, the third oldest college in the United States. Unconventional neighbor to the Naval Academy, the small liberal arts school traces its origins to King William's School, founded in 1696 by Sir Francis Nicholson, the governor who designed the Annapolis street plain. In 1784 the school was chartered as St. John's College "to perpetuate a succession of able and honest men." Women, too, since 1951. In the Great Hall of McDowell Hall (right) two dinners and a ball were given in 1824 to honor the visiting French general, the Marquis de Lafayette.

King William III looks on as a St. John's student defends his senior essay in an hour-long oral examination. The school limits enrollment to about 400 to allow such interaction between students and tutors. St. John's uses no textbooks, only the great books themselves. A sampling of the non-elective reading list: Homer, the Bible, Virgil, Shakespeare, Newton, Adam Smith, Jane Austen, Einstein, Faulkner, and selected decisions of the U.S. Supreme Court.

The first building on campus, McDowell Hall (left) was begun in 1742 as the mansion of colonial governor Thomas Bladen. Never completed, it was known as "Bladen's Folly" when acquired by the school in 1786. During the Civil War—when the Naval Academy moved to Newport, Rhode Island—the Union Army Medical Corps commandeered McDowell Hall as its headquarters.

Breakfast power brokers sit in the "Governor's Office," a booth at Chick and Ruth's Delly reserved for former Maryland governor Marvin Mandel (above, at right). This morning his guests are current chief executive, William Donald Schaefer, nearest the wall, and state comptroller, Louis Goldstein.

Confetti rains at midnight in the House of Delegates during the closing moments of the Maryland General Assembly. The house and senate meet for a 90-day session beginning in mid-January, but running the state is year-round business in Annapolis, also the seat of Anne Arundel County.

A sunset view of the harbor (preceding pages) embraces symbols of the city: the spire of St. Anne's Episcopal Church, the capitol dome, and the Naval Academy's Halsey Field House.

"A universal Mirth and Glee reigns in Maryland amongst all Ranks of People," a visitor observed of the colony's lively social scene in 1774, when card playing and cider drinking filled many evenings. Today chips fly at the annual July 14 Bastille Day casino party at the Maryland Inn (left).

First opened for business in 1784, the Maryland Inn was restored to charm by hotelier Paul Pearson (above, seated). Members of his staff represent the diverse professions needed to run the five historic Annapolis inns Pearson has renovated.

Hitting pay dirt, a mud beggar wins the favor and coin of the crowd at the annual Renaissance Festival in Anne Arundel County. Between shows he rinses off before renewing the competition: getting dirtier than his opponent. The late-summer festival re-creates a 1598 English village, complete with crafts-men, madrigal singers, jousters, sword swallowers, and a theater troupe.

Twin lighthouses strike a maritime theme at a Halloween party in the former St. Conrad's Friary, now a school and private residence on the north bank of the Severn River in Winchester.

Final resting ground for military
veterans and their families, Annapolis National Cemetery covers five
acres on West Street. The city's
annual Memorial Day parade begins
here and marches to City Dock,
where World War II veteran George
Grooms (above) awaits its arrival.

Neighbors unite for a yard sale on Bestgate Road on the north side of the city across College Creek.

Young Eastporters gather at a Chester Avenue playground. Separated from downtown Annapolis by Spa Creek, Eastport was an independent town until annexed by Annapolis in 1951.

The "painted ladies" of Annapolis (following pages), early 20th-century frame houses grace Conduit, Market, and Revel Streets near Spa Creek.

Spray-gun artist Norman Boston adds his touch to an electric guitar crafted at Paul Reed Smith Guitars. Custom built for such rock groups as the Doobie Brothers and Santana, the instruments have been praised by Carlos Santana as the "Maseratis" of electric guitars: "They're like finely tuned racing machines."

At the Maryland Hall for the Creative Arts, sculptors Debbie Banker and Joe Moss have freedom to pursue their visions. They are two of 17 artists-in-residence. With a heart for art, Annapolis supports a symphony, three theaters, and a ballet company.

A cascade of cornrows accents a young girl's beauty.

Just home from school, children begin their homework in the Robinwood Housing Project in Eastport.

Anne Arundel County holds more than 400 miles of waterfront property. Hugging the South River, the community of Riva (preceding pages) has roots as a summer retreat. The Annapolis region has been popular for millennia: Archaeologists trace human presence along the Severn River to 8,000 B.C.

Summer goes out with a song and a dance at the Labor Day picnic in Epping Forest. Overlooking Clements Creek off the Severn River, the wooded community began early this century as a collection of modest vacation bungalows. Now property values soar with the demand for land in Anne Arundel County, a waterfront haven within an hour's drive of Baltimore and Washington, D.C.

Once a golf course, the Downs on the Severn River (following pages) is being developed as a residential community where the price of a house can easily top a million dollars.

Fledgling ospreys, or fish hawks, prepare to leave their nest atop a Severn River navigation marker.

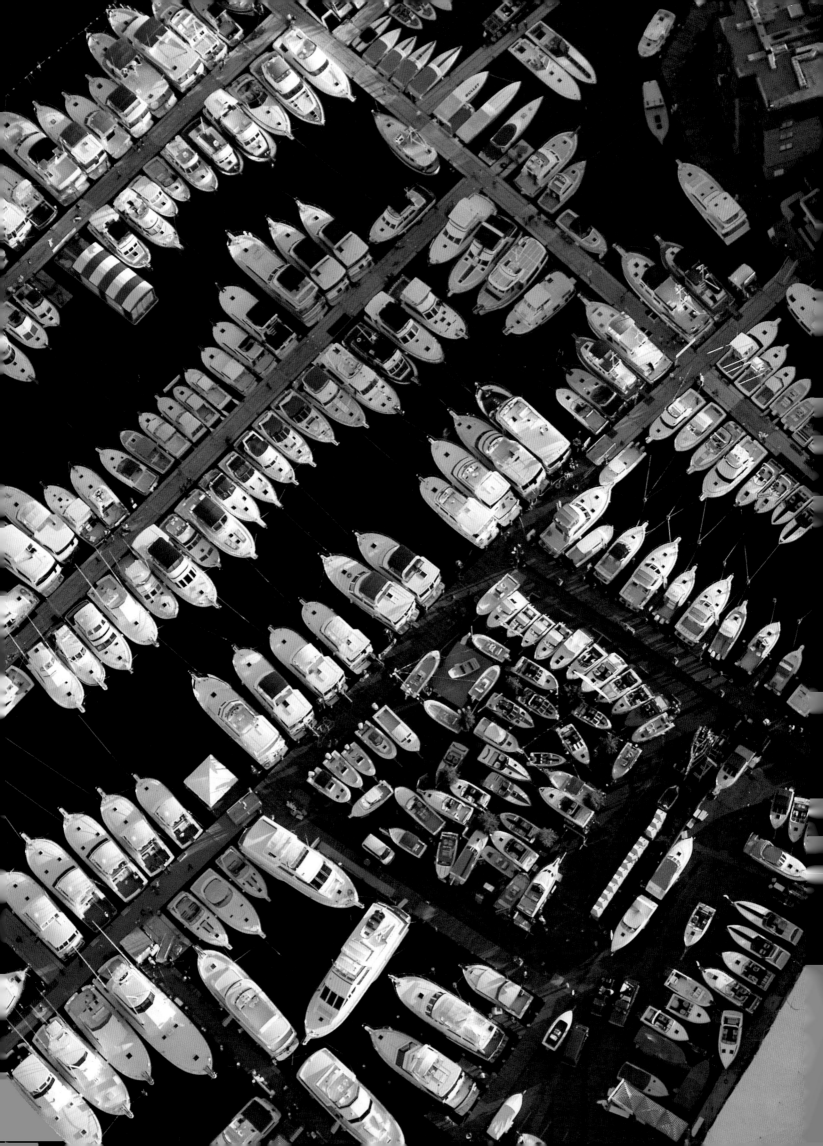

The country's largest in-the-water boat shows fill the Annapolis harbor each October. Held back-to-back, the United States Sailboat Show (above), and the United States Powerboat Show (left) together attract perhaps 100,000 people and pull more than 14 million dollars into the city's economy. Temporary docks accommodate some 500 boats; 150 more are displayed on land.

More than 200 businesses in Annapolis supply marine services. A high-rise garage for powerboats at Skip Bennett Marine on the South River (following pages) helps solve the perennial problem of docking space.

"Annapolis is still where the action is," says yacht designer Bruce Farr (above). The New Zealander has two America's Cup competitors to his credit, including his country's 1987 entry, *Kiwi Magic*.

The only boat still built in Annapolis, a Condor 40 trimaran is readied for launching in Eastport. As waterfront property values rocket, restaurants and condominiums have squeezed out boat/yards and other marine businesses unable to pay high rent. Now zoning laws prohibit non-maritime use of certain waterfront areas.

"Vessels of various sizes and figures are continually floating before the eye," chronicler William Eddis admired of Annapolis in 1769. On Whitehall Creek, a sailboat ghosts through October mist.

A face mask protects James Michie (above) from dust as he sands blue anti-barnacle paint on boat hulls. Such biocide paint may harm other marine life, warn some area environmentalists.

Hibernating in dry dock (left), boats will be cleaned and repainted for the spring season.

Early morning waterskiers (following pages) leave their signatures on the South River.

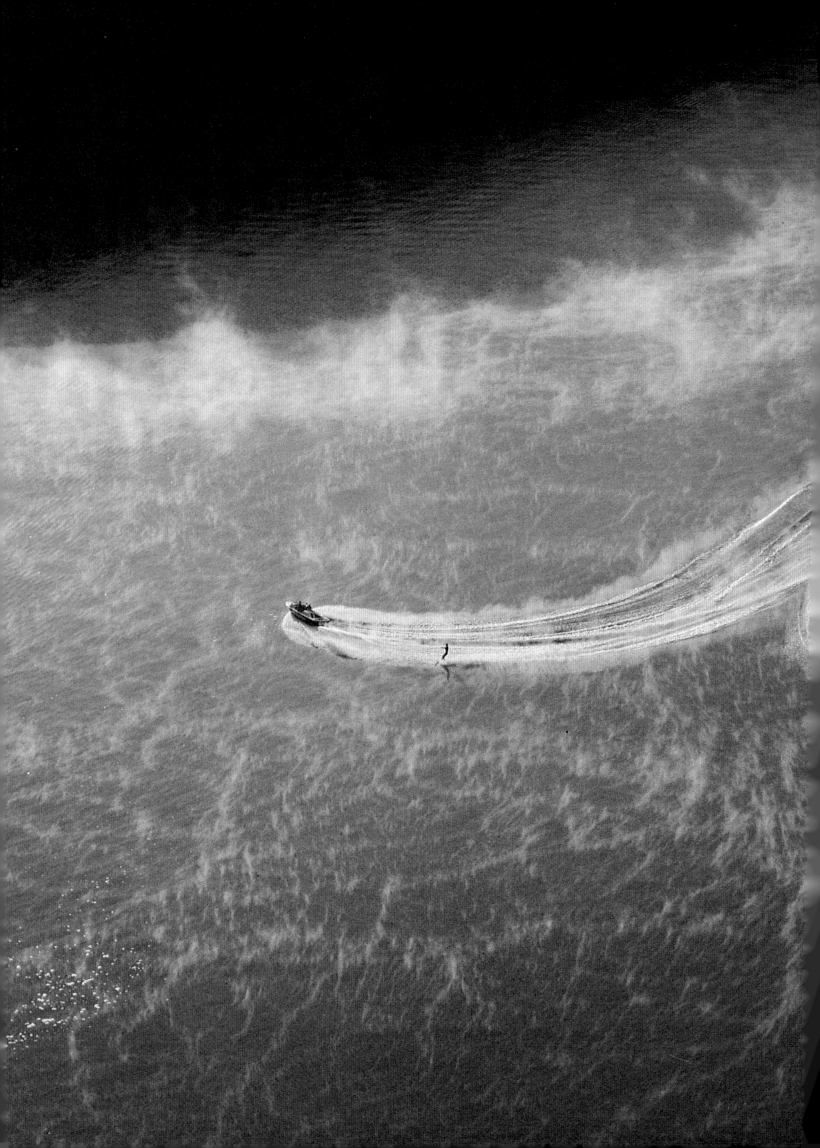

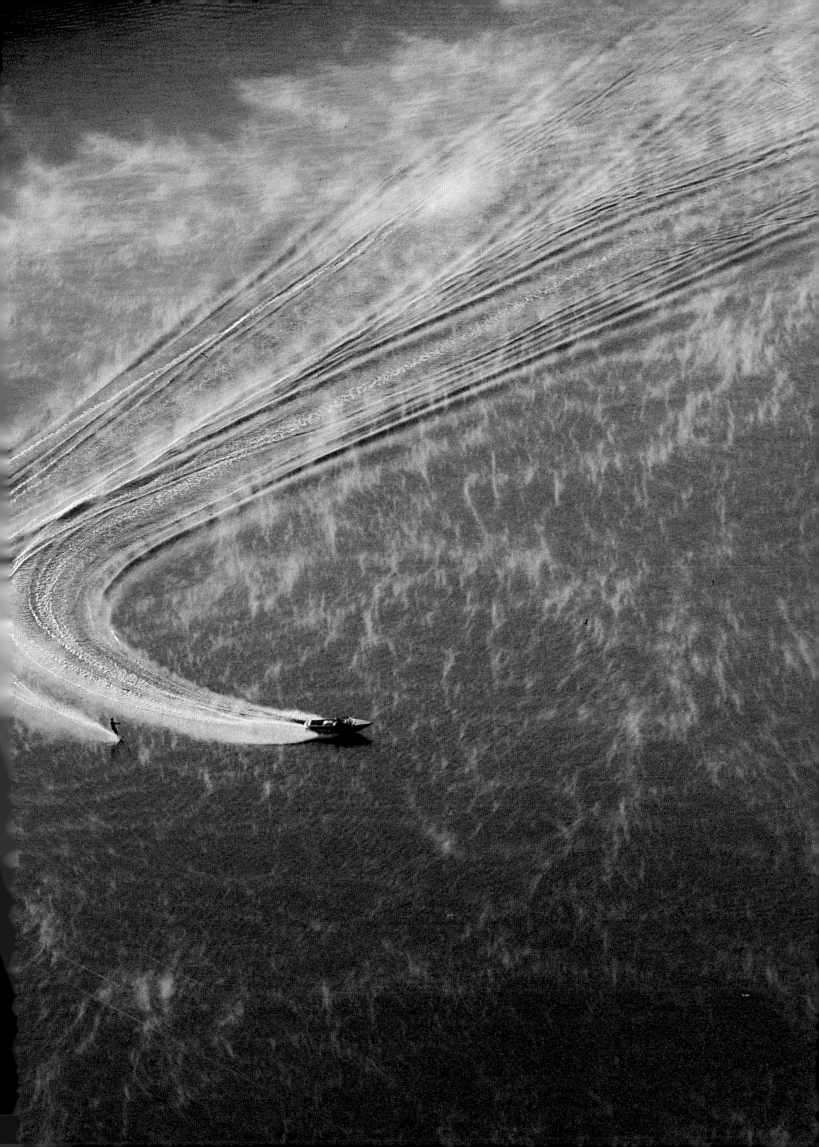

Like leaves on a tree branch, rowboats move with the wind at Sandy Point State Park.

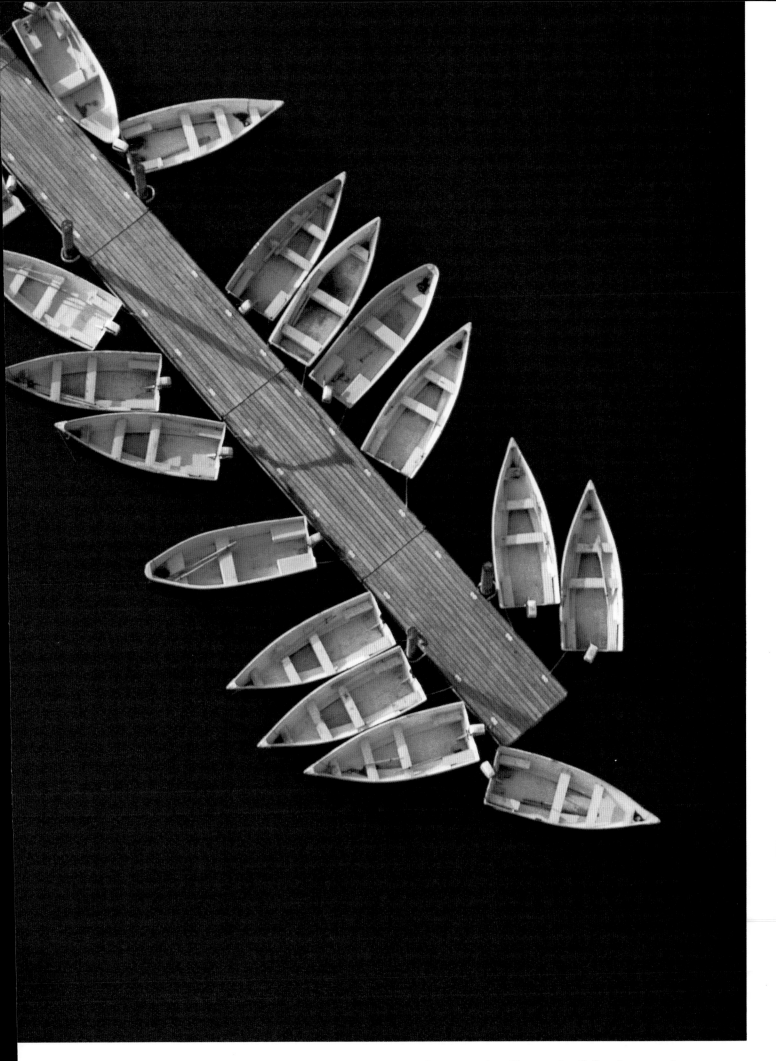

Below Annapolis, the South River flows into the Chesapeake (following pages).

Community spirit drives John Jason (above, at wheel) to collect food donated by supermarkets for the West Street soup kitchen run by the Christian Workers Mission. A retired contractor, Jason joined this endeavor "to help the poor and needy with food, clothing, and furniture." Special effort goes into preparing the Mission's Thanksgiving Day feast at Asbury United Methodist Church (right).

"Something like a barn raising," is how volunteers described the construction of the Annapolis City Playground (following pages). Families pitched in time and money to erect the prefabricated equipment.

Down-home democracy brings out voters in Highland Beach, a small community south of Annapolis. Incorporated in 1922, it is the only other municipality in Anne Arundel County. Every two years some 100 registered voters elect five members to the Board of Commissioners. Supervisor of Elections Dolores Queen checks the voter lists and later oversees the counting of ballots at her kitchen table.

Where the Chesapeake is at its narrowest (preceding pages), the William Preston Lane, Jr., Memorial Bridge links Anne Arundel County with Kent Island on Maryland's Eastern Shore. Named for the governor who initiated construction, the first span was opened to traffic in 1952; the second span in 1973. A Baltimore-bound freighter glides under the nearly 200-foot-high roadway.

Deftly netting a blue crab, Gordon Kolsox works his trotline. Baited with salted eel and secured to buoys at both ends, the trotline is drawn over a roller as the boat glides forward. As the sun rises, Kolsox heads up Whitehall Creek (following pages).

A patriotic streak has always run through Annapolis, the capital of the United States for nine months in 1783 and 1784. Dressed for celebration and honor, a Memorial Day Parade car rolls past Annapolis National Cemetery.

Designed by Gerard A. Valerio

Edited by Jane Vessels

Composed in Palatino by Composition Systems, Inc.,
Washington, D.C.
The face was designed by Hermann Zapf
for D. Stempel AG,
who issued the face in 1952.

Printed in Hong Kong by Everbest Printing Co., Ltd.
through Four Color Imports, Ltd., Louisville, Kentucky